STAR CHIL

CLARK ST]

**Other Cambridge Reading books
you may enjoy**

Truth or Dare
Edited by Tony Bradman

Tom Tiddler's Ground
John Rowe Townsend

Once upon Olympus
Jenny Koralek

**Other books by Jamila Gavin
you may enjoy**

Someone's Watching, Someone's Waiting

The Hideaway

Double Dare

Star Child on Clark Street

Jamila Gavin

Illustrated by Derek Brazell

CAMBRIDGE
UNIVERSITY PRESS

Cambridge Reading

General Editors
Richard Brown and Kate Ruttle

Consultant Editor
Jean Glasberg

PUBLISHED BY THE PRESS SYNDICATE OF THE UNIVERSITY OF CAMBRIDGE
The Pitt Building, Trumpington Street, Cambridge CB2 1RP, United Kingdom

CAMBRIDGE UNIVERSITY PRESS
The Edinburgh Building, Cambridge CB2 2RU, United Kingdom www.cup.cam.ac.uk
40 West 20th Street, New York, NY 10011-4211, USA www.cup.org
10 Stamford Road, Oakleigh, Melbourne 3166, Australia
Ruiz de Alarcón 13, 28014 Madrid, Spain

First published 1998
Reprinted 1999

Printed in the United Kingdom at the University Press, Cambridge

Typeset in Concorde

A catalogue record for this book is available from the British Library

ISBN 0 521 47624 0 paperback

Contents

CHAPTER 1

Flying Dreams

He thought it was a shooting star that furrowed through the night sky, leaving a trail of red sparks scattering like spray. He imagined the distant explosion – or was it a roll of thunder? Just the single, dreadful sound of the impact of an alien spacecraft crashing to earth. Then silence; a long, deathly silence.

If only . . . if only he could fly. He would leap into space and soar through the air until he found the giant crater which had been created by the crash, and maybe, emerging from the crater, there would be a magnificent, super iron warrior, who had come from the iron star to defend the world from its enemies.

If only he could fly . . . if only . . . He stretched out his arms and stood on tiptoe . . .

"Tarnie! What are you doing?" Isa hissed from the doorway of her brother's bedroom. He stood outlined at the window, in his pyjamas, with the swirling, metallic green Ironmaster cloak draped round his shoulders. Beyond their street, which was at the top of a hill, the city lay in a great spangle of orange street lights, glistening like a huge spider's web. The moon hung over the city, heavy and close; so close, he could see the mountains and craters; so close, he felt, that if he could just reach out and fly a little way, he would touch it – land on it – fly round it. He opened the window.

"Tarnie!" Isa reached in alarm for the light switch.

The force of the light was like a physical blow. Tarhunt reeled round, his hands up to his face. He had his glasses on. "What? What on earth . . .?" He took his glasses off, rubbed them and put them on again. "What . . .?" he mumbled, fighting his way out of his dream. Now he was awake. "Get out of my room!" he bellowed at his sister. "You know you're not supposed to come in without knocking. Get out – go on!" And he lurched forward for his pillow and hurled it at her. Isa fled.

Tarhunt fell upon his bed. His heart was thudding. He suddenly realised that he was enveloped in his cloak. He ripped it off, feeling foolish. He could hear his sister softly explaining, "Tarnie had another dream. He dreams he's the Ironmaster. He was sleep-walking in that cloak you made him, Mum, when he was younger. I thought he was going to jump out of the window."

Tarhunt heard the murmur of anxious voices as

8

his mother and father conferred. "It's all your fault," he heard his mother grumble at his father. "He would have grown out of Ironmaster by now if you hadn't kept it going. You men just never grow up."

Tarhunt couldn't help smiling. It was true. His father was a kid when it came to the Ironmaster. He still had the comics on order – he said for the children, but he was always the first to read them. He had one or two old *Ironmaster* comics too, and sometimes spent more than he should buying up back numbers. When their mother complained, he said, "It's an investment, dear. They're collector's items. If we run out of money and I have to sell them, we'll make a profit. You won't complain then, will you?"

"Hmm!" Mum had snorted. "You could argue the hind leg off a donkey."

Poor long-suffering Mum, thought Tarhunt. Why, she'd even had to put up with Dad insisting that the children were called after the *Ironmaster* characters. Tarhunt was the name the Ironmaster was given on the Iron Planet of UD.SIG5 and Isa was the cosmic goddess who helped him to fight demons.

Tarhunt turned on his bedside light, then switched off the glare of the main light. He carefully removed his glasses and got into bed again. Would he have tried to fly out of the window if Isa hadn't come in? Although his father would be an Ironmaster fan till the day he died, Tarhunt lost interest ages ago – until they moved here. Then, for some reason, he had begun to dream about the Ironmaster night after night; and because he dreamed about him by night – vivid, adventurous, flying dreams – he thought about him by day too. It got him into trouble at school, for instead of concentrating on his lessons, he day-dreamed that he was a superhero, flying to the rescue and saving the world.

His mother padded in, bare-footed and bleary with sleep. "You OK, Tarnie love?" she cooed. She bent over him all soothing and concerned, and tucked him in.

Tarhunt pushed the clothes off angrily. "I'm too hot, Mum."

She looked hurt.

"I don't like it here. I wish we could go back to St Paul's Road," he burst out. "I hate my school. I've no friends. Why did we have to move in the first place? I want to go back and be with Ian and Gareth. And I don't like this room. I don't like this house."

His mother sighed and sat on the edge of the bed. "Do you want to swap rooms with Isa?" she asked.

"No. Hers is worse. I want my old room. I want

to go back to St Paul's Road. I'll never like it here."

"Oh come on, Tarnie. It's a bit early to say that," reasoned Mum. "It always takes time to settle into a new home and school. This is a much better neighbourhood. Things will work out. You'll see."

Will they? Tarhunt wondered grimly. What did his parents know? He hadn't been bullied at his other school – and called names. But at this school, ever since his first day, he had put up with name calling and whispering and being tripped up – and even a bit of a fist-fight in the cloakrooms. He had been there a whole term now, but there was no sign of anyone being his friend.

"Isa is happy."

"Yeah! Isa is always happy." His sister had one of those friendly faces, with mischievous black on white eyes; her forest of tightly-plaited Afro hair bounced with jollity every time she moved her head. Isa was taller than the other girls in her class – she was even taller than most of the boys. Instead of teasing her, they seemed to adore her. It made Tarhunt feel sick. "Girls are different," he muttered.

"No Tarnie, not different. It's a matter of attitude. You've got an attitude," retorted his mother. "Isa just gets on with it. You skulk round like a bear with a sore head. No wonder you don't have friends. Just try a little harder." She bent over in a motherly sort of way and tried to stroke his head, but he pushed her off angrily.

"You don't know anything!" he snarled, and rolled away from her with his face to the wall.

"Hey, Tarnie." It was his father. "Don't take it out on your mother. Remember, you're a star child – a child of iron. You came blasting down to Earth from UD.SIG5 with special powers. You can fight off anything, can't you, mate?"

Tarhunt didn't reply.

"Goodnight, Tarnie," his mother said with a soft sigh, and switched off his light.

When he knew his parents had gone, he rolled over onto his back and lay with his eyes open, staring at the shadows on the ceiling. He clenched and unclenched his fists and punched into the darkness. If only he did have special powers. If only he could go 'Biff! Bam! Wallop!' and hurl his enemies to the other side of the universe. If only he could clench his fists and close his eyes and spin around in the playground as they all jeered at him, and turn into the Ironmaster.

Gradually, as he imagined himself swooping above his enemies and plunging into danger to save people, showing everyone how strong and brave he was, his eyelids began to get heavy and sink to a close.

Something swished past his face. He cried out. A dark shape, like a giant bird with outspread

wings – or was it a great cloak? – blotted out
the moonlight shadows on the ceiling, then
disappeared. Tarhunt didn't know if he was waking
or dreaming. He tried to sit up, but his body
seemed as heavy as lead and he couldn't move.
"Ironmaster?" He didn't know if he spoke the name
or just thought it. "I wish . . . I wish . . ."

CHAPTER 2

A Boy in the Window

"Oh the night, the night!" old Reggie Baxter sighed as he filled the kettle. Sometimes the night seemed so long, especially when he couldn't sleep. Now that he was old, the strangest things would wake him with a rush of memories: the throb of a distant motorbike, which could sound like those bombers in the war, flying out on a mission like iron geese in low formation; or the steady menacing whine of the V-bombers they called doodlebugs. He remembered being a boy in the war and how they used to listen . . . listen . . . listen to the doodlebug. "Which way is it going?" They would ask themselves. "Is it going to fly over our house? Keep listening!" For so long as they could hear the buzz . . . buzz . . . buzz . . . it was still flying through the air, on and on – and might pass over them. He remembered how the whining would suddenly stop. There was that moment of dreadful silence. Hearts would stop, for that was when the unmanned engine cut out, and the dreaded bomb would plunge down with an earth-shaking explosion to destroy whatever was beneath it.

As a boy, a whine from an engine would have

sent Reggie Baxter diving down under the bedclothes with a pillow over his head. Now he was a grandfather, a faraway motorbike roaring through the neighbourhood could still wake him with an instinctive jerk and then a sigh of memory. Unable to get back to sleep, he would potter along to the night-chilled kitchen and make himself a cup of tea.

Often, just through years of habit, he would stare out of the back window across the gardens, to the backs of the houses in Clark Street, remembering his childhood friend, Bill. He could see Bill's bedroom window – over there – first floor up, level with what had been Reggie's bedroom as a boy. They used to signal to each other at night with their torches. Then when the war began, they rigged a long, long piece of string across from Reggie's window to Bill's to make a telephone instead. They tied tin cans on each end and spoke into them, and their voices travelled along the string. Now Reggie's grandson Greg slept up there in his boyhood room. It was odd to think that Greg was the same age as he and Bill had been when they'd rigged up that telephone.

A new black family had just recently moved in to the Clark Street house – the Lomoteys. He was pleased to notice that a boy of about the same age as Greg – ten years old – had taken over Bill's old room. Reggie's mind drifted back to those days with

Bill: they had been the happiest of days, and the saddest of days. He slowly rubbed his gnarled working hands together. Then, gulping down his tea, he walked slowly back to his room.

In the back bedroom which had once been his grandfather's, Greg lay awake. He couldn't sleep either. He kept jumping up to get a drink of water. That meant he then wanted a pee so, no sooner had he got back to bed, his thirst quenched, than he was up again to go back to the bathroom.

Every time he went to the bathroom he had to pass Darrell's bedroom and, every time, a floorboard creaked loudly. Finally, his seventeen-year-old brother got annoyed and grabbed him as he went by. "You'd better keep a potty under your bed, you little twerp. Just stop creaking past my room. Every time you flush the loo, you wake me up," he raged.

So Greg lay there in the darkness, trying not to feel as though he needed the bathroom. He rolled over one way and shut his eyes tightly, then he rolled over the other way. At last, unable to stay in bed any longer, he got up and went to look out of his window. He looked over the back garden and beyond the fence to the back garden of No. 42 Clark Street.

A strange figure came to the window. It looked like a huge bird with a pointed head, and wings which spread right out. Then Greg realised it was a boy dressed up; a boy wearing a cloak and something on his head, spreading out his arms as if he wanted to take off into space. Briefly, the moon sailed out of the dark turbulence of a cloud and cast its light upon his upturned face and his outstretched fingers. He seemed to rise – as if on tiptoes – then the moon was engulfed again and the figure disappeared.

Fascinated, Greg went on staring across the darkened gardens. The orange glow of street lights punctuated the gaps in the long silhouette of houses stretching down the street.

Everything was new. They had only recently moved in to live with Grandad Baxter – his mother's father. Tomorrow, Greg was to start at his new school. He hadn't given it much thought over the holidays – there had been too much settling in to do.

As his mother had said bitterly, disaster strikes in threes. First Dad had lost his job, then they found Mum's job just didn't pay enough to cover the mortgage – so they had to sell their house. Finally, Grandad went and had a heart attack. Dad said it was a blessing in disguise. It meant that they moved into Grandad's house, to look after him, and it put a roof over their heads. But Grandad was not the easiest person to live with and it was a great strain on everyone.

At first, Grandad had been pretty well bedridden – so there had been a lot of fetching and carrying – but after a week or two, he was back on his feet and they all had to keep an eye on him.

He treated Dad like some kind of layabout, asking him almost every day, "Well – got a job yet?" As if to underline the point, every morning Grandad put on a grey bibbed apron and insisted on hobbling to his workshop at the bottom of the garden. He had been a carpenter by trade and was still happiest when he was sawing and lathing and making things.

Grandad seemed to be stranded in the past. He still lived as if it were wartime. He would never throw anything away. So there were drawers stuffed with paper bags and balls of string and plastic carriers; and he still made towers of coins for the meter – even though he no longer had any meters for gas and electricity – and a tower of coins for the telephone, even though he had his own and no longer needed to go down to the telephone box on the corner. If he saw anyone throwing anything away, he would chide, "Waste not, want not!"

Once Greg caught Darrell swiping a few 20p coins from one of the towers. "He won't notice," he muttered, seeing Greg's horrified face.

"That's stealing!" Greg hissed. "Put them back."

But Darrell just smirked and slammed out of the house.

"Don't slam the door!" came the inevitable

whine from Grandad's room.

Grandad had been employed since he left school at fifteen and couldn't understand why Dad hadn't got a job. He moaned on at him until, finally, Dad got fed up with being called a layabout, and said, "I'd best be on my bike and look elsewhere." Mum was upset and begged him to stay on a little longer and keep trying for jobs in the area, but Dad said, "There's nothing round here just now. I'll have to go further south." Very soon, he was gone.

After Dad left, Darrell had begun to get out of hand. He was such a big strapping lad – as tall as his father – and too much for his mother to cope with. He could be mean and bullying to Greg, but when Greg protested to his mother, she shrugged exhaustedly and said, "Just take no notice." Darrell warned Greg that if he went on being a tell-tale-tit he'd knock his block off.

Then Darrell said he wasn't going back to school.

"I'm sixteen now. I don't have to."

"But what about your A-levels?" Mum had wailed. She argued and reasoned with him in turn.

But he still refused.

"What will you do for a living?" cried Mum.

"That's right," Grandad supported her fiercely. "You're not going to be a parasite on me, I can tell you."

"I can get a living without all that A-level stuff," scoffed Darrell, and proved it for a while by getting a job at the local garage. But it didn't last long, and he got the sack for turning up late once too often.

So Greg would be setting off for school tomorrow on his own, and Darrell would be going to the Job Centre.

For the first time since they moved, Greg felt a shiver of anxiety. He'd never thought before about whether or not he would make friends. He'd always had friends – the same friends since the first year of primary school – but then he'd never moved before and never had to make any new ones. What if no one liked him? What if . . .? He looked across at all the darkened houses and wondered about the boy in the window. Perhaps he'd be a friend.

Suddenly, he desperately needed to go to the bathroom again. He crept down the passage. He succeeded in passing Darrell's room without treading on the creaky floorboard and was about to enter the bathroom when he saw a light coming from his grandfather's room below. He heard the choking wheeze of a cough. The wheeze seemed to go on for ever, and Greg wondered with alarm when Grandad would draw his next breath. He hurried downstairs. Through the open door, he saw the old man leaning on the windowsill, thumping his chest.

"You OK? Grandad?" asked Greg nervously,

wondering if he would get told off. His grandfather waved his arms in distress, and Greg stepped warily into the room. "Shall I get Mum?"

Grandad shook his head wordlessly, pointing to a glass of water by his bed.

Greg took the glass to him and his grandfather managed to gulp down a few mouthfuls. At last, nodding gratefully, he drew another breath, and then another and another.

"Thanks, lad," he muttered hoarsely, "I'll be fine now."

At that moment, the outline of the boy came back into the window opposite and stood there in the darkness.

"Look, Grandad! That boy across the garden. Do you know him? Looks a bit – you know – loopy – to me!" exclaimed Greg. "What's he got on his head?"

"That could be Bill over there," murmured Grandad, "still playing at being the Ironmaster. It's just like he used to be . . . The Ironmaster always wore an iron helmet on his head with a visor which could send out laser beams to kill his enemies."

"Who's Bill, Grandad?" asked Greg.

The old man smiled. "He was my best friend when we were lads together. Bill was crazy about the Ironmaster. I had to call him Tarhunt instead of Bill – that was the Ironmaster's name. Tarhunt Fe from the Planet of UD.SIG5!" Grandad chuckled at

the memory. "Bill's mother, though, was a holy terror. She would have given him such a hiding if she'd caught him reading *Ironmaster* comics. She thought they were bad and corrupting. My mother wasn't too keen either – mothers weren't then – but we were lucky. We had an American GI billeted on us in the war, who was hooked on the *Ironmaster* comics too. He bought every issue. When he was finished with them, he passed them over to me, and then I would sneak them to Bill. That's his old room over there – at No. 42. Everyone else was reading *Superman*, but Bill said *Ironmaster* was tons better. He was always dressing up and getting me to play Ironmaster games with him. Of course, Bill was always the Ironmaster." Grandad smiled, remembering. "The Ironmaster always wore iron. Even his cloak was made of iron. Bill had quite a time finding just the right material – shiny green to look as metallic as possible."

"Were you always the baddie then, Grandad?" asked Greg.

"Oh yes – I liked playing the Acid Man best. During the war, of course, the Ironmaster was fighting off the Nazis. We would play such games – just like the comic-strip stories, Bill would be fighting Hitler: catching bombs with his bare hands, beating off enemy aircraft and zooming up among the stars and planets to fight off alien invaders – me! Bill longed to be a child of the stars and always said he would be a pilot when he grew up. But he got ill ..."

The old man sighed and his voice trailed away. For a while, he and Greg stared at the boy in the window. The moonlight flooded round him, picking out his silhouette. He seemed to be preparing to fly. His arms were outstretched and his cloak swirled away in the darkness behind him.

"Did he get better?" asked Greg softly.

"No . . . no . . ." Grandad whispered sadly. "I thought he would. He took to his bed. I carried on smuggling in comics to him. Course, we were always on the look-out for Bill's mother, in case she found out, but she never did. Sometimes, I thought he was better. 'Come on, Tarhunt,' I'd say. 'Let's play Ironmaster!' And sometimes he did seem to be getting better. He would be up and off to school, cheery as usual – and we'd dress up and play Ironmaster. But then, quite suddenly, all his energy would drain away and he would take to his bed again. At first, his parents thought he was skiving off school. Everyone did – even the doctor, because he couldn't find anything wrong. That's why they thought he was putting it on. But not me. If I couldn't get Bill to play Ironmaster, then I knew there must be something wrong." He gave a wry laugh. "You know what?" He paused again.

"What?" Greg urged him on, fascinated by the story.

"Bill thought that there must be a lump of solid acid lying around, which had somehow got near to him – you know, like acid rock in the story –"

"No – I don't know. What was that, Grandad?"

"Well, Acid Man had this rock which contained

iron-eating acid, so powerful that if it touched iron it would start sizzling and melting away. It was the only thing that could destroy the Ironmaster. Bill got weaker and weaker, and he begged me to find the acid rock. I thought he was a bit bonkers." Grandad smiled at Greg and shrugged. "But just to please him, I did look. I looked everywhere, but I never saw anything like that; not even a rusty button, let alone some rock which was orange and glowing. Then one day, an ambulance came and took Bill to a hospital far away. I never saw him again."

The old man gave a shuddering sigh. "Acid rock," he whispered under his breath.

"He didn't really believe it, did he?" cried Greg. "I mean, he got better in the end, didn't he?"

"No, lad, no. He died. Doctors didn't know as much then. Today, he would probably have lived. For years I believed that lurking somewhere in that house in Clark Street was a lump of acid rock which had somehow been responsible and that if I'd found it, my friend wouldn't have died."

"Heigh ho!" The old man sighed and stared across the garden. Greg knew it was time to go.

"Goodnight, Grandad. I hope you won't cough any more."

The old man nodded and sat down on the edge of his bed. He would sit for a while, thinking and remembering . . . until a welcome drowsiness came over him once more. Then, without bothering to take off his dressing gown, he rolled himself into bed to sleep away the last hours until dawn.

Greg realised that he was really bursting for a pee now, so he tiptoed as fast as he could back to the bathroom. He managed to get into the bathroom without making a noise, but on the way back to his room he trod on the floorboard outside Darrell's room and it gave a long, accusing creak. He heard Darrell groan. Greg stood stock still, his face screwed up with disgust at himself for being so clumsy. But this time, Darrell didn't wake up. Phew! thought Greg as he made it back to his room again. That was close.

The house over the way was in darkness. No boy stood in the window. Greg got into bed and lay on his back, waiting for sleep. He liked looking at the wavering shadows scrawled across his ceiling from the old chestnut tree outside. Sometimes a car would go past and light from its headlights would squeeze in through the top of the curtain and then fan out in ripples over his head. Just before his eyes closed, he could have sworn that another shadow darted across the room, enveloping the room in a wide, flowing cloak. Briefly, he glimpsed a strange, bird-like head. Then it was gone.

CHAPTER 3

Friends and Enemies

Mum walked Greg to school on that first morning. Greg hadn't wanted to go. He had woken up with stomach-ache and was sure that he had appendicitis.

"I'm ill, Mum!" he wailed. "I'm not well enough for school."

"It's just nerves. You'll be all right once you're settled in."

"You're cruel sending me to school when I'm not well. I should report you to the Social Services!"

But Mum just laughed and prodded him forwards.

It wasn't far. Just round the corner into Clark Street, then down to the bottom and over the road. As they turned into Clark Street, Greg saw a girl and boy come out of No. 42.

"I wonder if that's the black family your grandad said had recently moved in," Mum said softly. "They're probably going to your school." She quickened her pace to catch them up.

The girl, who was older and taller than the boy, was striding ahead, urging her brother to walk faster. "Come on, Tarnie. Get a move on, will you," they heard her say.

But the boy – Tarnie, as she called him – seemed very reluctant. He kept dropping back, taking off his glasses and wiping them. He was quite short and rather thin, thought Greg. Definitely not the boy he'd seen at the window last night, who'd been whirling about and punching the air like a karate fighter. This boy's shoulders were hunched and his glance was furtive like a frightened rabbit.

Soon Greg and his mother drew level with them. "Excuse me, do you go to Hadley Middle School?" Mum asked politely.

The girl whirled round, her myriad Afro plaits flying like a merry-go-round. "Yes," she said shortly. Greg took a step backwards from her. She was tall. Taller than he was. Nearly as tall as his mother, and she looked ready to take on anyone.

"We're new round here," said Mum in a friendly voice. "This is Greg. He's just starting school today."

"Oh!" The girl's face softened and smiled broadly. "We're Isa and Tarhunt Lomotey. I'm Isa and he's Tarhunt."

"Don't call me that. I'm Tarnie," said the boy, looking embarrassed.

"Hey, Mum!" Greg hissed, tugging his mother's arm. "The Ironmaster's called Tarhunt. Grandad told me."

"Oh, don't tell me you're an Ironmaster freak as

well," said Isa. "My dad's crazy about Ironmaster. He collects all the comics. That's why we have these names."

"Yeah. And she's Isa, the Cosmic Goddess." Tarhunt threw his eyes up.

"We're new as well. That is – quite new," Isa chattered on. "We've only been here a few months. You can stick with us if you like," she told Greg.

"You look as though you're about Greg's age," Mum said to Tarhunt. "It's nice to know there's a friend just round the corner."

Greg squirmed. There she went again – trying to sort out his life for him. "Mum!" he protested weakly.

"Yeah!" answered Tarhunt, looking more interested. "I'm eleven."

"Fibber!" His sister denounced him firmly. "You're only ten."

"I'm nearly eleven, Isa. My birthday's only three months away," protested Tarhunt.

"That's the same as Greg," said mother. "He's nearly eleven too."

"Ten and three-quarters really," added Greg precisely.

"I expect we'll still be in the same class," said Tarhunt, giving him a quick grin.

Greg shrugged, but returned a sheepish smile.

When they got to the school gates, Isa shouted

cheerily, "See you later," and immediately plunged into a gaggle of girls, who all raced towards her with screams and laughter. Tarhunt seemed suddenly stranded and alone. No-one greeted him. To disguise the fact, he abandoned Greg and his mother and joined a bunch of boys jostling towards a side door, and disappeared into the school.

Greg and Tarhunt were in the same class, just as Tarhunt had predicted. The secretary took Greg in and left him to stand awkwardly at the front while his teacher checked the register. Dozens of eyes stared at him. He knew they were sizing him up. He caught Tarhunt's eye and managed to twitch a smile at him. The smile was noticed instantly, and everyone turned and looked curiously at Tarhunt as if to say, "How come you know each other?"

Finally, his teacher, Mr Byfield, introduced Greg to the class. Then he put him at a table with Andrew, Natasha, Polly and Naresh.

"Do you want to play?" shouted Andrew at playtime. Greg had gone to stand near Tarhunt and thought Andrew meant him. But Tarhunt didn't reply and Andrew shouted again.

"Who, me?" Greg was surprised. Yes, Andrew meant him, and headed the ball over to him. Greg returned it, then joined Andrew and Naresh and the others who were kicking a ball around. Tarhunt danced about on the edges, trying to join in. Greg kicked the ball to Tarhunt but, as Tarhunt dribbled it round preparing to return it, Andrew charged over and roughly elbowed Tarhunt out of the way.

"Hey, that's a foul!" cried Greg. But Andrew took no notice.

Tarhunt continued to hang around, but somehow the ball never came his way again. Greg seemed too caught up in the game to notice. After a while, Tarhunt drifted away.

A bit later, just before the bell went, Greg heard a group of children chanting, "Ironmaster needs a plaster. Kill Tarhunt, kill Tarhunt." He thought at first that it was yelled in fun. Then he saw what was happening. Tarhunt was running and dodging in and out, being chased. Surely, it was a game? Then Greg saw Natasha deliberately stick out a leg and trip him up. Tarhunt crashed heavily and Greg winced in sympathy. To Greg's surprise, instead of anyone helping Tarhunt up, they all jumped on him.

"Hey!" Greg rushed over. "Get off, you idiots!" He pushed the others aside. "Are you all right?" he asked Tarhunt, helping him to his feet. "Here!" He pushed Tarhunt's glasses back over his nose. "You nearly lost those."

"You a friend of his, or something?" Natasha asked scornfully.

"Didn't know Tarhunt had any friends. He's too

smelly," quipped Naresh.

"Do you know him?" asked Andrew, with a sneer. Everyone was listening for his answer and staring at him in a hostile way.

"Not exactly," Greg back-tracked defensively. "He lives near me, that's all. I only met him today."

Even though what he said was true, Greg could hear his words hanging in the air treacherously. He felt a quiver of shame. Tarhunt caught Greg's eye momentarily. "You too?" the look seem to say sadly.

Then Andrew jumped on Tarhunt's back. "Come on, Jelly Baby, fight me, fight me, fight me! I'm an alien mutant!"

"Tarhunt thinks he's the Ironmaster. Have you ever seen him in his cloak and that silly hat?" scoffed a voice.

Again Greg remembered the figure in the window. Tarhunt? He shrugged with uncertainty.

"His mummy made it for him when he was six. He's such a baby," sneered another.

"Having the Ironmaster's name doesn't make you the Ironmaster," cried Polly, scornfully. "He's nothing but a wimp. I can knock him down just like that," and she went and jumped on Andrew's back so that Tarhunt was almost brought to his knees with the weight of the two of them.

It looked as if the fight was getting completely out of hand. Greg looked round for the teacher on

duty, but she was seeing to a child with a nose bleed. Then a voice bellowed across the playground.

"Get off my brother!"

Andrew and Polly let go of Tarhunt and everyone scattered, yelling, "Look out! There's Isa!"

Isa marched furiously over to them like a sergeant major. "Leave off my brother," she bellowed. Then she grabbed Andrew by the collar and lifted him up till he was on tiptoe. "You leave my brother alone – you big bully!" she shouted right into his face and then pushed him away like a rag doll.

She spun round now to face the others, her hands outstretched with beckoning fingers. "OK, who's next?" But no-one wanted to be next. They all fell away and wandered off into other games.

"Wow!" Greg was impressed. He looked at Isa with wary admiration.

Her face that had been so friendly earlier was creased with anger. Her eyes flashed with rage and her fists were clenched at her side. Even Andrew wasn't going to mess with Isa. Mustering as much dignity as he could, he gave Tarhunt a sneering look and sauntered off with the gang.

Tarhunt adjusted his glasses and looked flustered. "Why don't you stay out of it, Isa?" he muttered. "I don't need you to fight my fights."

"It didn't look like it to me," retorted Isa.

The whistle went. Playtime ended and Tarhunt hurried in to school, ignoring his sister. As Greg passed her, Isa hissed, "I thought you were going to be a friend. But you're like all the rest. If I ever catch you laying a finger on my brother, I'll . . ." The noise in the cloakrooms drowned out the rest of her words.

CHAPTER 4

The Forbidden Room

After school, Greg went to Darrell's room and popped his head round the door. Darrell's long body was slumped on his bed. He was reading something, and looked up crossly. "How many times have I told you to knock before coming in?"

"Sorry," murmured Greg, edging closer to see what his brother was reading. "Hey! Is that an *Ironmaster* comic?"

"What do you want, twerp?" sniped Darrell. "You're always bothering me."

"Where did you get it?" exclaimed Greg, his eyes greedily reading over his brother's shoulder.

"None of your business! Now if you don't want anything, get out and leave me in peace."

"I was only being sociable," sighed Greg. "Where did you get it?"

"Mind your own business," snapped Darrell.

"Can I have it after you?" Greg persisted.

Darrell grunted incoherently and carried on reading.

"I was going to be friends with the boy in the next street along. He's called Tarhunt. That's the Ironmaster's name. Grandad used to have a friend who lived in that house – and he was an Ironmaster freak too – Grandad used to call him Tarhunt. Isn't that amazing? Did you know that? And Tarhunt's sister is called Isa – she's in the comics too. She's a Cosmic –"

"Go away!" snarled Darrell.

"I think the boy who's there now – Tarhunt – I think he's all right," Greg prattled on. "He seemed OK to me and we're both sort of new – he's only been at that school a term. But they hate him."

Darrell went on reading.

"There was a fight in the playground. You should have seen the way they all jumped on him."

"He's probably a twerp like you," said Darrell at last in a couldn't-care-less voice.

There was a pause. Darrell flicked through the comic and Greg stared out of the window, wondering about Tarhunt. He would like to be friends with him, but he also wanted to be friends with the others – especially Andrew. Andrew was strong and a leader. Only Isa was one up on him – and she didn't really count. If Andrew liked you, you were in; in with the gang, in with all the games. But if he didn't . . . "Why don't you like Tarhunt?" Greg had asked Andrew. "Because I don't – that's all," growled Andrew, and Greg had realised he couldn't be friends with both.

"Still here, twerp?" Darrell rolled over on his back.

"*Please* can I read it after you?"

"Go on then, you menace. It's baby stuff anyway. Go on, take it," and Darrell flung the comic across the room. "Now scram, will you!"

"Don't do that! You could have torn it!" protested Greg. He picked up the comic and smoothed out the pages. The iron grey, green and rusty orange colours of the *Ironmaster* comics glinted on the glossy cover under the heading, *The Ironmaster, Cosmic Warrior*.

He began to read. Whooosh! There was the Ironmaster up in the sky and shouts of "Look! Did you see that? The Man of Iron." Then there he was, standing supreme against the Acid Man's henchmen, his enormous arms outspread and hurling his deadly missiles.

"Get out of here, will you!" ordered Darrell. "You've got your own room now. Remember?"

Greg retreated, already absorbed. He spread-eagled himself, stomach down, on the floor of his bedroom and read the comic from cover to cover.

The Ironmaster is on the Moon in a life and death struggle with mutants. They aim a weapon of destruction at the Earth. The Ironmaster speeds in to stop them, with soaring cloak and a killer beam firing from his beaked helmet. There is a dreadful fight. The Cosmic Warrior is captured. The terrible creatures leer over him hissing, "You will die, Ironmaster, you will suffer . . ." One of the creatures holds something in its hand – something orange and glowing.

Greg wanted to read on. What was going to happen? Would the Ironmaster be able to fight off these enemies who have so many powers of their own? At the end of the last page he read, 'See next issue: Will the Man of Iron survive and return to

Earth in time to save London?'

"I must read the next episode . . . I must . . ." No wonder Tarnie loved the Ironmaster. Greg had never really read an *Ironmaster* comic before, but now he was hooked. He went rushing back to Darrell's room.

"Are there any others?" he asked his brother.

"How many times have I told you not to come barging into my room?"

"Sorry," Greg shrugged apologetically, "but . . . please, Darrell, tell me, are there any others?"

"Other what?" snapped Darrell.

"Other comics – *Ironmaster* comics."

"Loads."

"Where?"

Downstairs, the telephone rang. It was for Darrell, and with an impatient gesture which read as 'Stop bothering me,' he rushed off to plunge into deep conversation with a girlfriend.

Greg searched everywhere. He climbed up the rickety ladder into the attic and descended into the spidery lower regions of the cellars, but nowhere could he find any more comics. He wondered if Darrell was just fobbing him off. So he decided to be brave and ask his grandfather.

Grandad would be in his workshop as usual. He was forever fixing things or making things, as if determined to justify his existence. Only after supper would he go, regular as clockwork, down to the pub to have a pint of Guinness and a chat with his two regular mates. He would stay exactly one hour then come home again. It was obvious that he found it a strain, having his daughter and family all staying in his house. Any upset to his routines put him into a temper and he could snap your head off about nothing at all.

Greg usually stayed out of Grandad Baxter's way as far as possible. But after their chat last night, he felt more confident and, anyway, his desire to find the comics gave him extra courage. He planned a little speech, then went to the shed at the bottom of the garden. Gingerly, he pushed open the door. His grandfather was lathing a piece of wood, and didn't hear him immediately.

"Grandad . . ." Greg began.

The old man stopped and frowned. "What do you want?" he asked roughly. "I'm busy."

Greg was genuinely impressed with his grandfather's workshop. He'd never been in it before. He was amazed at the array of tools all neatly hanging on hooks. Where the house seemed so untidy, here there was perfect order.

"This is great, Grandad!" Greg exclaimed admiringly. "What are you making?" He came closer to the workbench.

"A telephone table. A chap at the pub wants

one," answered Grandad, his voice a little gentler.

"It's brilliant!" cried Greg. His eyes roamed all over, looking to see where his grandfather might have stored comics. But he realised that there would not be any junk lying around in this shed. It was far too organised. Everything had its proper place. There was nothing for it but to ask, "Grandad, you know you were telling me about those *Ironmaster* comics last night . . .?"

Grandad Baxter stopped in mid-action and looked up with a sudden smile. "Ah, yes. The Ironmaster – Cosmic Warrior. Yes, yes. He was the best!"

"Did you keep any of them?" asked Greg.

"Keep them? Of course I did. I collected them – kept every single one."

"You did?" gulped Greg, excitedly. "Where are they, Grandad? Can I read them?"

"Yes – if you can find them. It's been years and years . . ." His voice trailed off as memories overwhelmed him. "You'll just have to look around. In the cellars maybe. Now buzz off, will you. I'm working." Suddenly he was gruff again, and Greg left quickly.

"Where, where, where?" Greg wondered. He'd looked everywhere. Then he struck his head with his hand. "Of course!" he breathed.

When they moved in, Grandad had said they

could have the run of the house except for this one room, at the head of the second flight of stairs. He called it the box room and said it was the only room he didn't want them going into. "It's full of all the knick-knacks your grandma and I collected over the years. Nothing valuable, mind, just sentimental – so I'd rather you didn't go poking around."

"He's probably got all his love letters stored in there," Darrell had whispered, and set Greg off with a giggling fit. But Greg knew it wouldn't be long before Darrell did go poking around. He was that sort. Tell him not to do something, and he would have to do it.

I bet Darrell went into that room, thought Greg, the one we're not to go in.

After his phone call, Darrell had gone out. Mum was still at work and Grandad was busy working in the shed. Now's the time, thought Greg and went straight up to the forbidden door.

He tried the handle, but it was locked. Where had Darrell found the key? Greg went down to the kitchen and looked all around. Pity it wasn't orderly like the shed. The kitchen was a mess – a jumble of things. Mum had tried to introduce some order into the house, but it only led to quarrels between her and Grandad. "This is my house," he would say, "I have my own system. If I want to put jam jars on the mantelpiece and screwdrivers on the table and newspapers on the shelves, and a hammer and nails in the kitchen cupboard, then I will."

Greg's eye scoured the battered old dresser. Where would Grandad keep the key? There was a hook on the wall with a cluster of all sorts of keys. He took the whole bunch and raced up to the box room to try each one. But none of them fitted. He came back down and returned the bunch to the hook, disappointed.

Once again he stared at the dresser, his eye roaming across the landscape of coins, buttons, pins, letters, bills, pieces of paper with messages written on them, saucers without cups and an old, cracked teapot. His eye moved on, but suddenly shot back to the teapot. Something made him pick it up and shake it. It rattled. He took off the lid and tipped it upside down. With a clunk, out fell an old iron key.

Greg held it in the palm of his hand. He felt its cool weight. Yes. This could be it. He raced back up the stairs and fumbled at the keyhole. He slid the key into the lock. It fitted. He twisted it to the left; it turned easily. He hesitated. He remembered the story of Bluebeard's Castle and the forbidden room with its dreadful secret. I hope Grandad isn't a serial kil–. He stifled the awful thought and thrust open the door.

He stood staring. He felt uneasy, even a bit

afraid. There was a strong musty smell of old things which had been stored a long time: books, newspapers, mattresses and clothes.

The room was strangely dark. Jumbles of stored furniture blocked the window and shut out the light. His eye ranged over the confusion of belongings collected over a lifetime. All sorts of knick-knacks and odds and ends were piled onto chairs and into gaps between the furniture. If only he could see the comics, he wouldn't have to go inside – at least, he would hardly go in. He would

only have to rush in and out so fast that it wouldn't really count. After all, he prided himself on not being wilfully disobedient like Darrell. But there were corners he couldn't quite see into and bundles he couldn't identify: things stuffed into bags, magazines tied up with string and enough books to fill a library.

He took one step forward, then another. He listened. The house was silent. He rummaged clumsily around and felt like a thief. I'm getting out of here, he thought to himself, backing towards the door. Then he found himself staring at his shadowy image in the mirror of an old wardrobe. You haven't looked inside here yet, his mirror image seemed to say to him. Greg wrenched open the wardrobe door and leapt back, as if a skeleton might jump out. But only the pent-up odour of mothballs rushed into his face and made him clamp his hand over his mouth and nose.

He groped among the old-fashioned coats and shirts and pushed aside some hat boxes. Something glinted; something glossy. It was like striking gold. He gasped with the shock. He had given up hope; but there gleaming in the musty darkness were the grey, green and orange colours of . . . "Yeah!" Greg punched the air triumphantly. He was gazing at a great pile of comics, all entitled, *The Ironmaster, Cosmic Warrior.*

CHAPTER 5

The Nightmare

I have the power to conquer the world, but the wisdom not to do it. I could take anything I want, but it is better to give. I can fight anyone on Earth – even the very strongest – but I also help the weak. I am the Cosmic Warrior, the Ironmaster. Nothing can harm me . . . except . . . acid rock from Fe3 . . . It can burn through my iron-coated body if it touches me and leave me at the mercy of my enemies. But what is this weapon of destruction heading for Earth? It will kill millions of people. I must save them . . . yet I feel so hot. I'm burning . . . Aaaaah!

Tarhunt thrashed about in anguish. "Get it away from me!"

He struggled round the room, punching and kicking about. "It's burning me. It will destroy me. Get it away!"

"What? Get what away from you, Tarnie? Wake up! You're dreaming."

Isa, woken by Tarhunt yelling in his sleep, had come rushing in and found her brother in the middle of the room entangled in his duvet. His forehead glistened with perspiration and his eyes stared desperately. His Ironmaster cloak lay in a heap on the floor. Isa picked it up and shook it out as if she might shake out his nightmare.

"Where is it? Take it away! They've hidden it somewhere." Tarhunt rolled onto his knees and began tearing the sheets and pillow from his bed. "Acid . . . acid rock!" he panted. "Where is it?"

"Tarnie, what are you talking about? What are you looking for?" Isa tried to pull him to his feet, but he shook her off furiously as if she were his enemy.

"Get away from me! Get away! I must find the acid rock or I'll die."

Dad came in wearily. "What's going on?"

"Tarnie's having nightmares again," sighed Isa. "He's carrying on about acid rock again."

"This is going too far," muttered Dad. "It's just a story – a fantasy. Acid rock is just made up. It's all that stuff about a bit of rock – solid acid – which is the only thing that can burn through Ironmaster's iron skin – remember? You know – acid and iron don't go. Hey mate!" Dad hauled Tarhunt from out of the tangle of duvet while Isa straightened out the bed. "What's all this? Got some acid rock knocking around, have you? Come on! You're the child of the iron star. You've got the power to overcome anything."

"They were trying to get me," stammered Tarhunt.

Dad laughed. "Your mum's right. You have been reading too much *Ironmaster*. Better give it a rest, eh? Come on, lad. It's just fantasy. You know that." He put on the light. "Look! There's nothing here. You're in your own room. And there's no acid rock. Understand? It's just made-up. There's no such thing. Feel better now?"

Tarhunt got back into bed and Isa said, "It's awful sleeping next door to you these days. You shout and yell as if the demons of hell are after you. I think we should burn those *Ironmaster* comics."

"Don't you dare! Don't you dare!" Tarhunt nearly flung himself out of bed again in fury.

"Hey now, you . . . that's enough!" Dad pushed him back. "Course we won't burn them – but just don't read them at night before you go to bed. Read something less violent."

" Like Noddy," joked Isa.

"Ugh!" Tarhunt poked his tongue out at her.

"I hear from your mother that Mr Baxter has his daughter and her family living with him now. There's a boy called Greg, isn't there?" Dad chattered on, trying to take Tarhunt's mind off his nightmare. "Your age, isn't he? Same class too? That's good. Did you get along with him all right?"

Tarhunt grunted a nothing sort of answer.

"That's good, mate. It makes all the difference having a friend round the corner," said Dad, giving him a friendly punch.

"I wouldn't bank on it," snapped Isa. "Greg's the same as the rest of them."

"Stop it, girl!" Her father reacted sharply. "You're too hasty to judge. Give him a chance. After all he's new too, so he'll be feeling the same as you, won't he, Tarnie?"

"Yes, Dad," sighed Tarhunt, rolling over towards the wall.

"I've tried to teach you not to be so thin-skinned. Don't go looking for trouble."

"No, Dad." There was no point in arguing with him.

"Yeah, mate! Go to sleep and dream something nice. Dream about our holiday in Jamaica last year, when you went snorkelling. That was good, wasn't it?" His father rubbed his son's head with rough affection. "We'll go again in a couple of years when we've saved up some more money. Your Aunty Janice keeps begging us to come. Shall I leave your light on?"

"No!" growled Tarhunt, feeling humiliated. He hadn't needed a night light since he was six.

Isa and Dad went out, but left his door ajar anyway with the light on in the hall. Tarhunt lay staring at the ceiling. He was wide awake now, his body still tingling with the dread of his nightmare. He wished he could stay awake all night. He knew what would happen if he slept. He'd be the Ironmaster again – but weaker and fighting mutant aliens.

The mutants were evil. They believed in violence and thrived on death. They were smashing cities all round the world with their powerful weapons. Only the Ironmaster could stop them. But, somehow, they had got hold of a piece of acid rock from Fe3. They had hidden it somewhere near him; somewhere where he couldn't see its strange orange glow, yet where its rays could reach his body and turn his muscles to mush. His enemies were watching jubilantly as the Ironmaster's strength ebbed away.

Tarhunt sat up in bed. He stared around the room, looking for an orange glow. Then something glimmered through a gap in the curtains. It came from the darkness of the garden below. He thought he had seen something . . . he thought . . . He got out of bed. His legs felt wobbly and he shivered although he felt hot. He slung the Ironmaster cloak round his shoulders and went over to the window. He imagined that the night was full of energy, that superheroes were fighting silent battles with super criminals. He imagined them in dark caverns beneath the city, or shooting up into space to fight it out among the stars. He longed to be out there with them, but . . . he felt so weak all of a sudden.

There was a faint light coming from the window opposite. It bobbed around like a tennis ball in the room – Greg's room, he knew that now. What was Greg doing up in the middle of the night?

On an impulse, Tarhunt took up his torch and shone it across the gardens. On... off... on... off... For a while there was no response, then, suddenly, on ... off ... on ... off, the light flashed back from Greg's window.

For the first time since they moved here, Tarhunt smiled. He smiled in the darkness, and felt the weight in his body lighten for a moment. Perhaps he and Greg could be friends after all. He spread out his arms and swooped about in the window. Opposite him, Greg punched the air and dodged about, as if he and his torch were in a fight.

A wave of weakness made Tarhunt stagger. A sudden chill prickled over his skin like pins and needles. He flashed his torch on and off once more. Then, wearily dropping his cloak to the floor, he went back to the warmth of his bed and pulled the duvet tightly up to his chin.

He was almost asleep when something made him look up. His cloak rose from the floor. The figure was back. It stood in the centre of the room. It seemed to be looking for something. It rose up and up, and drifted to where it could look on top of the wardrobe. It glided past the window-frames and the bookshelves, then dropped down, down – the cloak billowing out like a vast mushroom – down to the floor which spread away into the darkness.

"Can't you find it, Ironmaster?" whispered Tarhunt. Somehow, this time, he wasn't afraid.

Tarhunt and Greg didn't look at each other the next day at school. Greg played with Andrew as usual, and Tarhunt hung around on the outside as he always did.

When Tarhunt brushed passed Greg in the classroom, Tarhunt said softly, "We should learn Morse code. Then we could flash proper messages. I've learnt how to do 'SOS'. It's dash dash dash, dot dot dot, dash dash dash. You know, long long long for S, short short short for O and long long long again for S."

"Yeah!" muttered Greg, "Everyone knows that." He was embarrassed about being seen talking to Tarhunt and hurried off to join Andrew. Tarhunt thought angrily that he wouldn't bother signalling to Greg. But that night, when Greg did flash 'long long long, short short short, long long long', Tarhunt answered back.

CHAPTER 6

Some Are Missing

Greg found that the best time to go into the forbidden room for more comics was straight after he got back from school. His mother usually wasn't home from her job, his grandfather was always working in his shed and Darrell was either out or in front of the TV.

Avidly, he followed the story of the Ironmaster, working through one issue after another. Often he read in bed, by torchlight so that he could switch it off quickly if anybody came. He had found that the comics dated back to the 1940s. There were stories about the Ironmaster fighting mysterious master criminals who wanted to take over the world – evil gangsters who tried to pump his body with bullets, but they only bounced back off his powerful chest; he put bar-room bullies in their place and exposed corrupt politicians and cheating businessmen. Week after week, he played cat-and-mouse games with his arch-enemies: the Acid Man, Delilah, an evil Earth woman, and the diabolical Cyclotron.

Always, there was a deadly fear that other enemies would find out how to overcome him, that enemy aliens from other galaxies would come with their own super powers: criminals who had been banished from distant planets but who, like him, had found their way to Earth. Most of all, he feared his deadly enemy, the Acid Man, who had promised to track him wherever he went – all over the universe if necessary – to pay him back for handing him over to the Cosmic Guardians. The Acid Man had the one thing the Ironmaster dreaded – acid rock. Even one small grain could burn right through his skin, and a rock the size of an egg could kill. His tall, leering, fearsome body, dominating the page, made Greg shudder with terrified delight.

Every night, he and Tarhunt flashed torches at each other, pretending that they were sending secret messages. Tarhunt usually had on his Ironmaster's cloak. Greg watched him, fascinated. It was as if Tarhunt knew what Greg was reading and acted it out. Sometimes, when Greg got up in the night to go to the toilet, he would see a cloaked figure, standing in the window opposite, looking as if he might leap out and fly up into the stars.

They became strange night friends, but hardly looked at each other at school. Greg was always with Andrew and Naresh. But once, when Andrew, Naresh and some others jumped on Tarhunt in the playground and began to bully him, Greg pulled them off saying, "Oh leave off, won't you!"

The comics had been stacked in order so, night after night, with his torch aimed at the pages, Greg pounded on through the stories. He began to think of nothing but the Ironmaster and to dream of the Ironmaster. Then suddenly there was a gap – a break in the story. Greg looked at the dates and found that some of the comics were missing. He grunted in frustration. Could they have got separated? Had Darrell got them? But Darrell denied all knowledge and wasn't interested any more.

Greg went back into the Forbidden Room to have a really good look for the missing comics. That's when he got caught.

"I thought I told you this room was out of bounds to you." Grandad loomed in the doorway. He looked furious and his voice quivered with anger.

"Sorry, Grandad. I . . . was looking for those *Ironmaster* comics you said you had . . ." Greg got to his feet, shamefaced. "I looked everywhere. Then I thought they might be in here . . . Sorry, Grandad. I've found them now. They were here and I've been sorting them out for you . . ." His voice trailed away and he dropped his eyes.

"Oh, you have, have you?" The anger had died in his grandfather's voice.

There was a long silence. Greg looked up. His grandfather was staring at the pile of comics. "Good heavens, lad, you really did find them!" He came into the room and took one gently in his hands.

"Ironmaster! After all these years, my goodness gracious . . ." He began to read.

"Grandad," interrupted Greg, warily. "You've got every single issue up to 1950, except for about six missing, all in a row. Why would that be?"

His grandfather sat down on a chair, examining the rest of the pile. After a while, he said, "You're right, lad. Six missing. Now why . . . why?" He

shifted his glasses and read on for several minutes, sometimes chuckling, sometimes breathing out with excitement. Then he said, "Of course! Bill! I expect Bill had them. Remember I told you he got ill? I used to smuggle my *Ironmaster* comics in to him. He'd read them secretly – mostly at night, with his torch. When he'd finished, I'd smuggle them out again. I'd never throw them away. Oh no – that would have seemed criminal. I would never throw *Ironmaster* comics away. I liked collecting; I liked things to be in sets and in order."

"So, can you remember what happened to the six that are missing?" asked Greg. "I think they're the ones where Ironmaster goes back to the Iron Star."

"Oh Lordy, yes I can," Grandad sighed. "It must have been the last time I saw Bill. He was ever so poorly. I took over six or so comics to cheer him up. Bill said he had a hiding place for them so his mother wouldn't know, but he never told me where it was. Then he got taken to hospital all of a sudden – and that was it. He never came home, and I couldn't exactly ask his mum for my comics back, could I? Poor Bill . . . He was my best friend. I used to sleep in the bedroom where you are now. We used to signal to each other with our torches from our bedroom windows . . ."

"Hey, I do that too, Grandad," exclaimed Greg. "I'm friends with that boy over there now. The one who lives in Bill's old house. And guess what his name is. Tarhunt, after the Ironmaster! His dad's like you. Crazy about the Ironmaster! He likes to be called Tarnie, but they tease him like anything at school."

"Tarhunt." Grandad shook his head in amazement. "Well I never..." he said, almost to himself. "A star child on Clark Street. Just like Bill. We even made our own telephone link – you know, tin cans and string stretched across the garden. 'Warriors of the Iron Star!' Bill always used to end his messages with that. Poor Bill..." Grandad subsided into a melancholy silence.

Greg stared out of the window across to Tarhunt's house. Funny to think that the six missing comics could be there – and acid rock, too? Could there really be some hidden somewhere?

"You could ask that mate of yours if he's come across the comics," said Grandad, getting gruff. "Now scram, and don't let me find you in here again."

The swipe Greg received across the head as he dashed past was more friendly than hostile.

The next day, Greg caught up with Tarhunt and Isa on their way home. They were surprised to find him in their company as he always ganged up with Andrew and the others after school, and went to mess about in the park before tea.

"What do you want?" demanded Isa sharply.

"Nothing," muttered Greg, kicking a stone along the gutter. "Just going home."

"Well, walk on your own," she snapped.

Tarhunt was more friendly. He lunged at the stone too and, for a while, they kicked it back and forth between them in amiable silence. Then Greg said, "Is that an Ironmaster cloak I've seen you in?"

"Yeah!" Tarhunt looked sheepish and braced himself for a taunt or jibe, but Greg said, "It's good. Did your mum make it?"

"Yeah – she made me a whole outfit, but I grew out of it. I only wear it sometimes now – just for fun."

"Do you read the comics?" asked Greg.

"My dad does, and I read his. He collects them."

"That's what my grandad did – when he was a kid. He's got all the copies right from the very beginning."

"Wow!" breathed Tarhunt, impressed. "They must be worth a fortune!"

"What? Comics worth a fortune?" frowned Greg in surprise.

"Dad said that the other day, a man sold one comic from 1948 for a thousand pounds!" cried Tarhunt. "Dad said that one day his would be that valuable."

"Phew!" exclaimed Greg. He wanted to ask

Tarhunt about his grandfather's lost comics and whether Tarhunt had found them, but he suddenly felt awkward. What if they had found them? Wouldn't they just say, 'Finders Keepers'? Especially if they were valuable. So he said nothing, except . . . there was one more thing. Just before Tarhunt and Isa peeled off into their gate, Greg couldn't help asking, "Are you all feeling OK?"

"What?" Isa looked as if she thought he was a bit soft in the head.

"There's no-one ill in your household is there, or anything like that?"

"Of course not. Why should there be?"

"Why are you asking?" puzzled Tarhunt.

"Just being polite. Polite people always ask after your health, don't they?"

"Yeah – but I didn't especially put you down for a polite person," commented Isa sharply, herding her brother indoors.

When he got home, Greg made a big mistake. He knew it as soon as the words left his mouth. He told Darrell about the comics, and all about how Grandad, when he was a boy, had lent some to his friend Bill. It was so unusual for Darrell to listen to anything he was saying, that Greg just blathered on.

"There are six missing. You haven't got them, have you Darrell?" asked Greg. "Tarnie's dad collects comics. Tarnie says they'll be valuable one day. He says a man just sold one for a thousand pounds – can you imagine? A thousand pounds for a comic! Grandad thinks the old missing ones could be in Tarnie's bedroom . . ."

That's when Greg realised he had made a mistake. Darrell said softly, "Hey! One comic worth a thousand, did you say? Then our pile is worth thousands and thousands. A collection would be worth a fortune. I never realised comics could be valuable. Fancy our old Grumps having a fortune right under our noses!" Greg could almost see the pound signs flashing in his brother's eyes.

"We could sell them. We'd be millionaires! I could get my motorbike," Darrell breathed excitedly. "No – why bother with a motorbike? I could get a sports car – a Jaguar or a Lotus or a Lamborghini! Hey! Think of that!"

"Don't be daft!" Greg felt uneasy at Darrell's enthusiasm. "Anyway, they're Grandad's comics, not yours. It would be his money – that's if he wanted to sell, and I don't think he would . . ." Greg's voice faded with uncertainty.

"But he wouldn't know, would he?" hissed Darrell. "He never goes through all that junk in there, and you wouldn't say a word now, would you, little brother?" he added menacingly.

"Anyhow, a collection's no good if some are missing," retorted Greg defiantly.

"Then it's up to you to find them, isn't it, twerp?" said Darrell with a greedy, determined look. "Starting with your friend. Look around his house. In the cellar or the attic or somewhere."

"But I'm not friends with Tarnie – not really," protested Greg. "And I never go to his house."

"Then you'd better hurry up and make friends. Why should the Lomoteys have them? They're more ours than theirs – and we sure could do with the money – couldn't we?" said Darrell, his face right up to Greg's.

Greg dropped his eyes miserably. "I suppose so."

"You suppose so! You know so. So get on in there," said Darrell, giving him a punch which wasn't quite playful.

"Hey! That hurt!" winced Greg, rubbing his shoulder.

"Don't be a wimp," jeered Darrell, and went out.

CHAPTER 7

Friends by Night

Greg went to the library. He asked the assistant to help him to find a book on Morse code.

"It'll be in the encyclopaedia, under 'M'," she said.

She pointed to a shelf containing about ten volumes of encyclopaedias. Greg looked up 'M' for Morse. There it was: the whole alphabet laid out in dots and dashes. He copied it out on a piece of paper and took it home. Then he began to work out a message for Tarhunt.

That night, he flashed rather laboriously, 'I like the Ironmaster.' But Tarhunt didn't understand, of course, and could only flash back 'SOS'.

"Sorry," Tarhunt whispered in school the next day. "I didn't understand your message."

"The code's in the encyclopaedia," Greg hissed back in an 'everyone should know that' kind of voice, and walked off.

But Tarhunt didn't have an encyclopaedia. An uncle had taught him 'SOS' but nothing more. Greg could flash all kinds of messages, but 'SOS' was all Tarhunt could do.

Anyway, he was confused by this secret

friendship. Greg was keen enough to flash torches through the window at night, but he ignored him completely at school. They hardly talked to each other. Tarhunt no longer tried to join in with Greg in the playground, and Greg was usually a passive onlooker when Tarhunt got teased. Only if the bullying got really rough did Greg interfere and drag the others off.

Yet later that day, Greg again caught up with Tarhunt and Isa on their way home from school. Tarhunt was pleased, but Isa was suspicious.

"What do you want?" she asked shortly.

"Nothing," answered Greg.

"Well don't get too close, you might catch a disease."

"Oh! Are you ill?" asked Greg with alarm.

"Goodness me! This is a turn up for the books. Walking home with us, interested in our health. What's brought this about?" asked Isa with heavy sarcasm.

"Shut up, Isa! We're friends, Greg and me, aren't we, Greg?" cried Tarhunt.

Greg shrugged. "I wanted to show you this." He pulled out a bit of paper. "I've written out the alphabet in Morse code for you."

Tarhunt was delighted. "Hey, man! That's wicked! We can get this thing going really good, eh?"

"Get what going?" cried Isa suspiciously. "What are you two up to?"

The two boys just looked at each other and laughed. "It's strictly private!" exclaimed Tarhunt.

When they reached Tarhunt's house, Tarhunt begged Greg to come in.

Greg was almost going to agree, when suddenly a voice shouted, "Hey, Greg! I've been looking for you. I thought you were coming over to my place." It was Andrew.

"I'm coming!" called Greg, wishing Andrew hadn't turned up and seen him with Tarhunt. He hesitated and looked uncomfortable. "See you!" he said to Tarhunt with a wry grin, as if to say, "Sorry, mate. That's how it is." And he crossed the road to Andrew.

"I thought you and Tarnie were friends," taunted Isa.

"Shh!" pleaded Tarhunt. But the disappointment nearly choked him.

Greg pretended he hadn't heard.

"Well?" Darrell pushed into Greg's room a few days later.

"Hey! You're supposed to knock!" protested Greg.

"Heard anything about those comics?" demanded Darrell.

"No. Not yet. I'm not really his friend yet," muttered Greg.

"Come off it. You can't be trying properly."

"I am, but . . . well, it's not that easy. I am trying."

"You're not trying hard enough. Look here, twerp . . ." Darrell leaned forward menacingly and twisted Greg's ear between his fingers. "Get on with it. Make friends. Find those comics. I've got someone lined up to buy the collection – and he says it's the early comics that are the most valuable. If you don't do it, I might have to find other ways."

"You're a bully! I hate you!" cried Greg, his eyes smarting with pain as Darrell pinched his ear even harder. "If Grandad knew . . ."

"He'll never know unless you tell him; and you'd better not do that or I'll have you shredded. Just get on with it. Make an effort."

"All right, all right!" Greg wriggled away. "I'll try tomorrow."

But Tarhunt was not in school the next day. Greg wondered what was up. He heard Mr Byfield mutter, "Oh yes. Tarhunt's ill," when he came to his name on the register. But Greg couldn't ask what kind of 'ill' he meant.

Tarhunt wasn't in school the next day either. Greg wanted to ask Isa what was wrong with him, but she always scowled when she saw him and turned away. Was it acid rock that was making Tarnie ill? That's what Greg wanted to know. Was it there, secretly glowing orange somewhere in his room, slowly sucking away his strength?

That night, when a torch flashed from Tarhunt's bedroom, Greg was really pleased.

. . . . / . / . _ . . / . _ . . / _ _ _ / 'Hello,' the flashes spelt.

Greg dashed out of bed and flashed his torch back: 'Hello, Tarnie.' At least he's well enough to play the torch game, thought Greg with relief.

'What's up?' Greg flashed to Tarhunt.

'Don't know. I feel weak.'

'Acid rock,' Greg flashed.

There was a long pause from Tarhunt.

'When are you coming back to school?' asked Greg.

'Monday. Perhaps.'

The weekend came and went. On Monday morning, Greg saw Isa on her way to school – but alone. Greg caught up with her. "How's Tarnie?" he asked.

"What's it to you?" she asked suspiciously. "I don't understand you, Greg. I've seen you at school. You never play with Tarnie. I don't think you're really his friend at all. What's your game?"

"I am his friend!" blurted Greg. "Ask Tarnie. He knows."

"Tarnie's sick."

"Sick? What do you mean, sick? It's just a cold, isn't it?"

"No, it's more than a cold. It's what I said. Sick. Ill. Poorly. Got it?"

"When is he coming back to school?" asked Greg.

"Dunno. We don't know what's wrong with him. He's got no energy. Everyone says he's skiving off school, but he's not. I know him. He couldn't lie around in bed all day unless he was ill – he just couldn't do it. Usually he can't keep still for five seconds." She frowned with anxiety. "Anyway, the doctor's coming to see him again."

"Acid rock!" breathed Greg softly. "I wonder if it's . . ."

"What are you on about?" cried Isa.

"Oh nothing," murmured Greg.

Again, after school, Darrell interrogated him. "Well – have you made friends with him yet?"

"He's ill," said Greg.

"Good. Then you can visit him. That's the perfect excuse," said Darrell.

"I was going to anyway," retorted Greg.

When Greg flashed his torch that night, he told Tarhunt he would come and see him. Tarhunt flashed back eagerly, 'Yes.'

The next day, after school, Greg took a bundle of his grandfather's *Ironmaster* comics and called at Tarhunt's house.

The door was opened by Isa. "Oh, it's you," she said coldly. "What do you want?"

"Can I see Tarnie?"

"I dunno." She looked as if she wanted to slam the door in his face, but instead she yelled "Mum!" very loudly.

Mrs Lomotey appeared, drying her hands on a tea cloth. She was a big, tall woman – as tall as Isa. Her face broke into a wide smile when she saw Greg.

"You're Tarnie's friend, aren't you?"

Greg saw Isa throw her eyes up with contempt. She knew what went on in the playground. She knew how Tarhunt was always being teased and bullied and that Greg had hardly ever stuck up for him. No, Greg went with the crowd, and Isa thought he was a coward.

But their mother beamed with pleasure. "Tarnie's told me about you. Go on up! I know he'll be pleased to see you!"

Tarhunt, in pyjamas and dressing-gown, was sitting at a table, across which were spread sheets of white paper and colouring pencils. He looked up and took off his glasses. His eyes widened with pleasure at the sight of Greg. "You came!" he said, beaming.

Greg didn't know Tarhunt could draw. His walls were covered with his drawings and they were all of the Ironmaster and the Ironmaster's enemies.

"Hey! They're good!" cried Greg admiringly. "Look, I've brought you some of my grandad's old *Ironmaster* comics to read. I'll want them back though, OK? You'll have to be really careful with them, they're part of a collection."

Tarhunt gasped when he saw the comics. He looked at them closely, then said, "Wow, these are really old – the earliest. If my Dad saw these, he'd go mad." He took the comics from Greg, handling them carefully, as if they would break. "A collection would be worth thousands."

Trust Darrell to be right about that, thought Greg bitterly.

While Tarhunt began to get absorbed in the comics, Greg got up and walked around the room, wondering where Bill, a sick boy, could have hidden a bunch of comics all those years ago. He looked up and down and examined corners. He tapped the walls and listened for a change in sound.

"What are you doing that for?" asked Tarhunt with a laugh.

"Oh, I just wondered whether you had any secret hiding places behind the walls. Some old houses do," answered Greg, as if it were all part of a game.

"No such luck! We haven't anything interesting

like that. There's only the attic, full of junk. One day, Dad says he'll turn it into a spare room," said Tarhunt.

Greg walked over to the window and looked out. He could see his own bedroom over the way. "Hey, Tarnie! Why don't we rig up a telephone between our two rooms – you know – with string and tin cans!"

Tarhunt looked excited. "Will it work?"

"My grandad did it when he was young. Let's try."

It took a bit of doing – finding a strong piece of string that was long enough, and stretching it all the way from Tarhunt's bed, across the gardens, over the fence, between the branches of the chestnut tree into

Greg's room. Greg did most of it alone because Tarhunt was too weak. But at last it was done, and it worked.

They decided to communicate by Morse code at night and use their tin-can telephone by day.

"Hello, Tarhunt, this is Argon," Greg called through his tin can after school the next day. Greg had always been secretly envious that Tarhunt was named after the Ironmaster. 'Greg' is a boring name. What could I be called? he had pondered. It was Tarhunt who suggested Argon. "That's the iron bird who helps the Ironmaster in some of the stories. Yeah – Argon's not bad for a name."

So that's what Greg called himself when he was playing with Tarhunt. "Hello, Tarhunt, this is Argon. Have you anything to report?"

"Yeah!" shouted Tarhunt through his tin can. "I saw an alien spaceship filled with mutants heading towards Earth. We'd better be ready for them. They're out to take over the world. Let's go! Warriors of the Iron Star, over and out."

Every day, after school, Greg called in on Tarhunt, always taking some comics with him. He always greeted him with "Hi, Ironmaster." And Tarhunt would reply, "Hi, Argon. Let's go! Warriors of the Iron Star, over and out."

Greg began to like Tarhunt – really like him. The more he liked him, the more he hated himself for secretly hunting round his room for the lost comics – especially when he looked so ill. For whenever he could, Greg peeped in a cupboard or furtively opened a drawer or looked on a shelf.

"You know what?" Tarhunt told him confidentially one day. "It's as though there's some acid rock in my room somewhere – burning me up." Tarhunt lay back on his pillows, exhausted.

Greg felt a stab of fear, remembering Bill. "So you think it's acid rock too?" mused Greg.

"What do you mean? Who else thinks it's acid rock?" asked Tarhunt, anxiously.

"I mean – like the comics." Greg knew it would be stupid and unfair to tell Tarhunt about Bill.

Tarhunt sighed and lay back on his pillows. "I told Mum I wanted to leave here and go back to our old home."

"If there is acid rock in your room, where could it be?" asked Greg, warily.

"I don't know," Tarhunt's voice sounded suddenly weak. He lay back on his pillow and closed his eyes, as if the whole effort of talking had become too much.

"Where's a good hiding place in this room where they could hide acid rock?" Greg probed with concern. "You've got to get better, otherwise the world will be destroyed," he teased.

Tarhunt looked at him. His eyes were uneasy –

even afraid. "I don't know where they could hide it," he said. "I mean – it's bright orange. You couldn't exactly miss it. I've been racking my brains about where it could be ever since I began to feel like this."

"I'll have a look round and see what I can find," murmured Greg with a shudder of uneasiness. What was he? A friend or a spy?

He searched carefully through Tarhunt's room, half the time not knowing whether he was looking for a make-believe acid rock or hidden comics.

"I can't find anything," he said softly. But Tarhunt didn't open his eyes, and Greg quietly left the room.

As Tarhunt got weaker and weaker, Darrell became increasingly impatient to find the missing comics.

"Well," said Darrell one morning, "have you and that twerp found anything yet?"

"Not yet," said Greg with lowered eyes. "But I'll tell you something. Tarnie's not a twerp. He really is my friend."

"Who cares," snorted Darrell, "so long as you find the comics? After all, they belong to us. Are you trying hard enough?"

"Yes, I am!" snapped Greg with a burst of anger. "But he's not well, and I hate you!"

"You won't hate me when we sell those comics for thousands of pounds. I don't think you'll hate me then, little brother!" sneered Darrell.

CHAPTER 8

Break-in

Tarhunt felt weaker than ever. His limbs wouldn't work for him. It was as if his body was on fire. This must be how the Ironmaster felt when his enemies secretly placed scattered grains of acid rock near him. In the night, in his dreams, the Acid Man slipped a piece of the deadly rock into his room. The Acid Man's voice spoke menacingly, "Now I have you in my power, Ironmaster! Now I will destroy you!"

Tarhunt awoke and tried to move, but couldn't. What's ha – happened? I feel so hot . . . Is there acid rock somewhere around? He tried to sit up.

Isa felt scared. Was Tarnie going to die or something? She felt scared because she could see her mum and dad were scared too. At first, everyone had hoped it was just Tarhunt skiving off because he wasn't that happy at school. But now it was clear he really did have something wrong with him. The doctors wanted to do more tests and scans and things like that, and they took him into hospital for a few days.

She felt lonely. Her mum and dad spent all the

time they could over at the hospital, and they had sent her to live at her gran's on the other side of town. Her gran was very deaf, so it wasn't easy to have a conversation with her. There seemed to be no-one she could talk to. No-one whom she could tell how afraid she was.

Everyone said how grown-up Isa was. At first, her mother had told her in a harassed sort of way, "Do the shopping, love, and cook your gran a meal, and you'll have to see yourself to school on the bus," and on and on . . . but soon Isa found herself taking charge.

Worst of all was that Mrs Lomotey had asked Greg's mother if she would feed their cat, Millie.

"But, Mum . . ." Isa wailed. "Why can't I do it? We don't have to ask *them*! Millie will hate it."

"I don't want you going to an empty house and then getting yourself over to Gran's afterwards. No, Greg's mum promised to do it – or there's Greg and Darrell too."

Isa groaned with disgust. "I bet they'll forget."

Friday was swimming day, and when on the Thursday Isa realised she had left her swimming costume back at home, she was glad of the excuse to go and get it. Then she could see Millie. I bet no-one's given her any cuddles for days, she thought fretfully. She decided to go straight after school. She wouldn't be that late – and Gran probably wouldn't notice anyway.

No-one was around when Isa got to her house. No-one saw her go in through the front door except Millie, purring with pleasure. "I hope they've been feeding you," whispered Isa, hugging her. "I wish I could bring you to Gran's but she hates cats."

Isa went upstairs to her room and began to hunt for her swimming costume. "Where is it? Where is it?" she muttered, rifling through her cupboards and drawers.

Then something stopped her dead. A sound; a furtive, secretive sound. Someone else was in the house. The sound came from downstairs. She crept out of her room on to the landing. It might only be Greg or his mum come to feed the cat. She peered over the banisters. She saw the top of a head. It wasn't Greg. It was someone taller, older. He disappeared before she could see properly.

In terror, she crept into Tarhunt's room and quietly shut the door. Her breath panted out in gasps. She wanted to scream. She wanted to scream her head off. Yet somehow, she clammed her teeth together and tried to make herself think. What could she do? She couldn't ring for help, because the telephone was downstairs. She tiptoed to the window. It was too high to jump from. Perhaps if she waved, someone would see her. She saw a movement in Greg's house. She waved her arms frantically – but no-one seemed to notice. It was then she saw the tin-can telephone.

When Greg got back from school, Darrell wasn't at home. Greg sighed with relief. It was good to have him off his back for a while.

"He's out with his mates again," sighed Mum, who was in before him for once, "but at least he fed the Lomotey's cat for me."

"You didn't send Darrell to feed the cat, did you?" Greg was aghast.

"It was very nice of him to offer," smiled Mum. "Shows he can be responsible when he wants to."

Oh *Mum*, thought Greg despairingly, don't you know your own son yet? How long was it since Darrell had done anything 'nice' or 'responsible'? He knew exactly why Darrell wanted to feed the cat.

Greg wandered uneasily up to his room. He stood at the window, staring across to Tarhunt's room. There was no sign of anyone, but he could see the cat sitting inside on the windowsill. Oh no! Don't say Darrell had locked it in when he went over to feed it.

Suddenly his tin-can telephone began to rattle and jiggle about. Someone was tugging at the string. Tarnie? Was Tarnie home again? He grabbed the tin and yelled into it. "Tarnie, is that you? Are you home?"

"Greg! It's me, Isa!" She was whispering but in a kind of shout. She sounded frightened and the string which linked the two of them across the back gardens quivered with tautness. "Someone's in the house!"

Oh no! Don't say Darrell's still in there, Greg groaned to himself. "Are you sure? Did you see someone, Isa?" he yelled in alarm.

"Yes, it's a man. He's upstairs. It must be a burglar!"

"Stay where you are, Isa," cried Greg into the tin can. "I'm coming over right now."

"No, call the pol–"

But Greg had already gone.

The back door was open when he reached Tarhunt's house. Greg stepped in quietly. "Darrell?" he whispered sharply. He was scared. This was stupid. What if it wasn't Darrell, but a real burglar? He listened, his nerves tingling. He crept further into the house and stood at the bottom of the stairs. He couldn't hear a sound. He glanced quickly into the downstairs rooms. "Darrell?" he hissed again. No answer. He could see Tarhunt's room through the banisters. Isa had shut the door. The other doors were open. His ears strained for the slightest sound – but there was nothing. Then he noticed something strange. A chair was positioned under the attic trap-door in the landing ceiling. Greg looked up. The door had been slid open. He heard a slight movement. Someone was up there. "Darrell?" He tried to call as softly as he could.

The bedroom door opened a crack. Isa peered out – her eyes wide with terror. She dragged him inside.

"Isa?" he whispered. He wanted to voice his suspicions. "It could be D–"

"He's up in the attic – I'm sure of it" hissed Isa. "It must be a burglar. We should phone the police."

"No, no!" gasped Greg, horrified. "I mean no – not here. He'll hear us. Let's do it from my house."

"OK. Let's make a dash for it then," said Isa.

They tiptoed to the door, and Isa turned the handle very, very slowly. They peered out onto the landing and up at the open attic door with the chair underneath. They listened all the time for any sound.

"Miaow!" The cat's piercing, hungry cry startled them. It galvanised Isa into action. Before Greg could stop her, with a kind of war cry, she leapt up onto the chair, slammed shut the attic door and bolted it.

They heard a muffled cry and the sound of someone banging as they hurtled downstairs.

He crouched in the dusty darkness, swearing and cursing; yelling and shouting to be let out. There was only one thin shaft of light from a narrow window in the roof. It left a pale circle on the floor, like a moon floating in a dark sky.

He knew perfectly well it was Isa and Greg who had locked him in. What did Greg think he was up to? Just let him wait. As soon as he was out of here, he'd show him; he'd pay him back. He'd twist his ears round till they faced the other way.

As he raged and plotted fiendish revenge, he slowly became aware of a far corner of the attic, low under the eaves beyond the skylight; a darkness darker than night. It seemed to be moving towards him. It undulated like a great, black wave: at first just rising and falling and lapping against the beams, but then billowing out and subsiding as if some wind puffed into it. It began to extend itself further and further into the middle of the attic. Glints of green and rusty orange shone briefly as it passed through the shaft of light. In the midst of the darkness and the glinting colours, there seemed to be the figure of a boy.

Darrell stopped his ranting, his anger suddenly extinguished. The figure was becoming clearer, growing bigger and bigger – and the boy became a man . . . like a knight in armour, but the metal of the armour flowed like water . . . From within the strange beaked helmet, green eyes looked at him and burned. Darrell inched away, back and back, finally crumpling against the wall. He covered his head with his hands.

"No, no! Don't hurt me! I'm sorry, I'm sorry!"

Greg and Isa had rushed through the kitchen and out through the back door. Suddenly, Greg stopped dead in his tracks. "No, no!" he groaned.

"What's up! Why have you stopped? Come on, let's get the police!" hissed Isa.

"No, no! I can't." He turned to go back.

"Greg?" wailed Isa with amazement. "What are you doing? Where are you going?"

"Back inside."

Isa followed Greg back into the kitchen.

Yes, he had seen it – as a blur in their frantic dash from the house. "Look!" Greg pointed to the table.

"I don't understand." Isa was still whispering, and tugging at his arm.

"The key-ring. It's got a 'D' on it," muttered Greg, his mouth going dry with shame. "And it's got your back door key on it – the one your mum gave us."

"So what?" cried Isa.

"I think we've locked my brother Darrell up in your attic."

Greg began to explain about the lost comics.

"You rotten little traitor. You great lumping idiot. You filthy spy." She raged on and on, her language getting worse and worse. "I always knew you weren't a true friend of Tarnie's," shouted Isa and, this time, furious tears spilled down her cheeks.

CHAPTER 9

Discovery

It was Tarhunt's first night in his own bed in his own room since getting back from hospital. He felt normal again. The doctors had said it was all very peculiar, probably some unknown virus which had affected him and now gone as mysteriously as it had come.

When Tarhunt had suggested to the doctors that 'acid rock' might be the cause, everyone had smiled and said, "What an imagination!"

Later, though, he'd overheard one of the doctors saying to his parents, "Of course, his state of anxiety has made it worse. Anxiety can make a person really ill. I understand he gets bullied at school? Bullying is enough to make anyone ill. You'll need to have that stopped."

Finally, he had been brought home. Tarhunt shivered. Half of him was excited and half full of dread. What about the acid rock? What if it was still in his room? What if he started to feel weak all over again?

The tin-can telephone jangled. It was Greg trying to get in touch. Tarhunt wouldn't answer. He hated him, now that he knew Greg had only wanted to be his friend so that he could find the missing comics.

When Greg tried later to communicate with his torch, still Tarhunt didn't answer.

'Hi, Tarhunt! It's good to have you back.'

No reply.

'Are you really better?' flashed Greg.

Still no answer.

'I'm sorry. I wasn't just looking for the comics.' He flashed the message out laboriously. 'I was looking for acid rock. It can kill the Ironmaster. I didn't want it to kill you.'

The pause continued. Greg signalled again. 'Tarhunt, remember the Ironmaster always wins. We'll find that acid rock and get rid of it for ever.'

Tarhunt lay back and pulled the sheet up to his chin. He closed his eyes grimly. Sadness overwhelmed him. He dropped off – or, at least, he thought he did – but then he was awake again. Something made him open his eyes. Something made him feel wide awake. He fumbled for his glasses and jammed them on. A figure had come into his room, wrapped in a long green cloak. "Isa?" No, how silly. It wasn't Isa. As the figure threw off the cloak he saw it was a boy. "Greg?" No, it wasn't Greg. Greg had light curly hair and blue eyes. The boy turned towards him and, although the light was out, Tarhunt now saw him clearly. He was rather thin and bony, with a narrow face. He had straight dark brown hair, parted at the side, and was wearing blue striped flannelette pyjamas. He carried a torch and a comic. He came over to the bed – Tarhunt's bed – and, as if it were empty, just climbed in. Then Tarhunt's amazement turned to utter terror, as the boy lay back on top of him and passed straight through him like thin air, just as if he wasn't there! With fright paralysing him completely, Tarhunt watched the boy roll over onto one elbow, switch on his torch and begin to read the comic – an *Ironmaster* comic.

Tarhunt was icy cold. Fear, as sharp as a knife, scored through him. He didn't know his heart could pound so hard. Was this real or a dream? Was the boy a ghost? Or was he, Tarhunt, the ghost? For he didn't exist for this boy; Tarhunt was invisible to him.

Tarhunt lay there motionless, sliding in and out of consciousness, not daring to move or even breathe.

He heard footsteps on the stairs. His mother was coming. Tarhunt tried to rouse himself, but his body was numb. Mum! Tarhunt opened his mouth to cry out, but not a sound escaped.

The other boy reacted like a shot, though. Without getting out of bed, he grabbed the comics, leant out and thrust them under the bed. He hung over the side for perhaps five seconds, then rolled back, snapped off the torch and disappeared.

Tarhunt fainted or slept – it hardly mattered which. When he awoke, it was getting light. He lay on his back looking round the room, still haunted with a feeling of dread. His eyes roamed around, resting on familiar objects in his room for reassurance. Then he remembered his dream. Or was it a dream? He froze in sudden horror. Was there a boy in the same bed? He forced himself to turn his head and look to either side of him. No. There was only himself. No boy lay propped up on one elbow, reading comics by torchlight. He stretched out a hand and patted the space. Would he feel a body? No, just a cold sheet and the pillow and the blanket.

After a while, the grey light turned to yellow, as a soft morning sun penetrated the curtains. Feeling bolder, Tarhunt tentatively rolled back to the side of the bed where the boy had lain. He bent over and looked under the bed as the boy had done, and pulled aside the carpet. He lay like that for a few moments in deep thought. Then he saw the floorboard.

Half dreaming once again, Tarhunt was the Ironmaster. But it was a nightmare. His enemies had captured him and he had no strength to get away. Any minute now he would be blown to bits by an acid bomb.

He could see the trigger wire which controlled the mechanism – if only he could reach it. With every last ounce of energy left in his weakened body, he stretched out his hands, his fingers wavering like thin grass blowing in the wind; extending, feeling, reaching for the wire. He had to get closer. Close enough for the laser beam in his visor to burn through the wire. Yes. He had got it. He felt it between his fingers. Just in time, he dragged it over his face. He pointed his visor and stared at the metal. The rays of heat fused the trigger connection. BOOM! A massive explosion shattered the blackness of space and blew the evil rock into a trillion particles.

He could feel strength flooding back into his body. "I did it! I'm free! Now I can return and carry out my mission!" He soared upwards into the stars, then headed for Earth.

Tarhunt was gasping for breath. "Argon, Argon!" He scrambled to the bottom of the bed, dragging his limbs which felt as though they were chained down. He crawled across the floor to the window. He rattled frantically at the tin can and shrieked down the piece of string. "Argon, Argon! Greg! I've found them! I've found the comics!"

CHAPTER 10

Destiny

"You're right! They're here!" whispered Greg. He was lying flat on his stomach under Tarhunt's bed. He had eased up the floorboard, and there, still rolled up as Bill had hidden them forty-five years before, were six *Ironmaster* comics. Greg's hand shook with excitement as he brought them out and tenderly blew the dust from them.

They carefully spread the comics out on the bed. "It's got the bit where the Ironmaster manages to blow up the acid rock and save his life," murmured Tarhunt. "Look!"

The boys stared silently at a full-page picture which glowed a deadly, rusty orange. Then Greg shut the comic with force. He shuddered. They looked in wonder at the colours of the comics – the grey, green and orange had hardly faded in all that time.

"What shall we do with them?" asked Greg.

"Take them away." Tarhunt recoiled from them. "Take them back to your grandfather. They belong to him."

Greg bent down again and peered into the dusty darkness beneath the floorboard. He was about to put back the loose board, when he noticed something glinting in the thick dust.

Greg stretched out his hands, wriggling his fingers nearer and nearer.

"Greg?" Tarhunt called out in alarm. Greg had become strangely silent. Tarhunt couldn't even hear him breathing. Tarhunt rolled over and looked over the edge of the bed. Greg's arm was under the floorboard up to its elbow. "Greg? What are you doing?"

"I've found something!" Greg's voice sounded odd and muffled.

Slowly, Greg reappeared. He uncoiled himself from the floor and knelt at Tarhunt's bedside. He had something clenched in his hand.

"What is it?" Tarhunt whispered.

"I don't know yet. Do you want to see?" Greg looked afraid. He flicked open his fingers quickly – just so they could see it once.

It could have been a cheap, garish stone fallen out of some costume jewellery but, in that brief second, it looked like a small, evil piece of burning rock from the depths of hell: orange, glowing, malevolent.

Tarhunt fell away from it in terror. "Get it out of here!" he gasped.

Greg snapped shut his fingers and ran from the room. He ran down the stairs, brushing past an astounded Isa. He ran out into the street. Where should he go? It was only glass, wasn't it? Where should he go? Where should he throw it just in case . . .? He balanced on the edge of the kerb – looking both ways along the street. Then he saw the drain.

Greg closed his eyes, feeling the object inside his clenched fist. Did he only imagine it or did it feel hot, hot enough to burn? He forced his fingers open. Surely it was just a stone? But it glowed with a bright orange light. His gaze was drawn into its very centre – deeper and deeper – until it was as if he saw the last moments of the Iron Star bursting into flame: exploding in vast shafts of fire and smoke and rock and water; spewing out across the universe like a million atom bombs; the heat searing into him, burning him up.

With a cry, Greg dropped it.

The orange stone rolled, and poised – just for a fleeting second – on the metal rim, before plunging through the grate. Far below he heard it hit the surface of the water, and imagined it in the watery blackness, sinking into the oblivion of the city drain.

Greg slumped onto the kerb. He stared down through the grate. There was nothing to be seen.

"It's gone," said Greg. "You'll be all right now." He had returned to Clark Street.

Tarhunt got out of bed to greet him. Already he looked stronger and more upright. He raised his right hand in salute and studied Greg's face. "Friends?"

"Friends." Greg held up his right hand. There

was a faint red mark on it, like a burn scar. He looked at it. It didn't hurt. He showed it to Tarhunt. They laughed out loud and struck palms. "Warriors of the Iron Star!"

Reggie Baxter shuffled as quietly as he could through the sleeping house, down to the kitchen to make himself a cup of tea.

Funny how some days are magic, how everything can go right. The boys' father had returned today with good news. He had managed to get into a small building firm back in the area and there was even a chance they might take Darrell on as well, to train in plastering and carpentry.

Yet, while the family was overjoyed, Reggie was filled with deep sadness. It was as though it was only yesterday that his best friend Bill had died. They had found Bill's old hiding-place and the comics were still there. And that stone . . . Bill had been so frightened of acid rock . . . If he'd found that stone all those years ago – and Reggie had destroyed it – might Bill have found the will to get better and lived? The thought filled him with anguish. He and Bill might have grown old together. He would always miss his friend.

At least the comics were complete now. He would never sell them; some things were beyond price. Darrell would learn that one day. Perhaps he had already learnt something after being caught in the attic in Clark Street. He was lucky that the Lomoteys had decided not to take it any further.

But something else had happened in that attic – something which had changed Darrell. Quietened him down. Made him more thoughtful. He hadn't told anyone, but you could see it in his eyes. Something had happened.

Reggie Baxter took his hot cup of tea and stood at the window, staring out into the night. As much as Greg and the family had disrupted his life for a while, he realised now that he would miss them too, when they left – especially Greg.

A torch flashed from Bill's window at No. 42 Clark Street. Reggie smiled and reached for his torch, but before he could click it, an answering flash beamed out from his old bedroom upstairs. "Bill?" Ah yes. Of course it wasn't Bill, but Greg's friend, Tarnie – and Greg was already waiting to reply.

A rush of wind shook the old tree outside, rattling its leaves. A great dark shadow swooped over the house. A thin ray of bright light swept over the garden and for a moment, the light of the moon was blotted out by a wide, flowing cloak. He seemed to hear a voice echoing through the night:

"Warriors of the Iron Star!"

"Bill?" Reggie whispered.

"I think we're going to be all right now, Ironmaster!"